"My first thought upon my Journible arriving was wow! I plan on purchasing at least one of these for each of my girls. I would like them to have a copy of handwritten Scripture from me. Possibly in the future they will want to purchase their own copies and use them personally. The 17:18 Series would also be good to use in your homeschooling. They are great for copy work and handwriting practice. Plus you will be using the Word of God with your children. The Word of God never returns void."

—Melissa, mother from Trenton, Florida

"I really enjoy this resource because it causes me to slow down and to think about what I'm reading and writing, to meditate on aspects of the Word that I otherwise might just skim. It's true that I don't have time to read as big a chunk of Proverbs every day that I usually do, but what time I do have is rich with new insight and meaning."

—Jasmine, homeschool student and daughter of Voddie and Bridget Baucham, Spring, Texas

"The Journible I am currently using covers the books of James, 1 and 2 Peter, 1–3 John, and Jude. I have spent the last two weeks slowly making my way through James, and it has opened my eyes to the Scriptures like never before. Not only am I reading the Scripture, but I am writing it, meditating on it, answering thought-provoking questions, and reflecting on how my life should change to reflect what the Scriptures teach."

—Jeremy, pastor from Jacksonville, Florida

The 17:18 Series

Journible® through

James

This book belongs to:

_____

Given by: _____

Date: _____

REFORMATION
HERITAGE BOOKS

James
© 2011 by Full Quiver LLC
www.fullquiver5.com

Published by
Reformation Heritage Books
2965 Leonard St., NE
Grand Rapids, MI 49525
616-977-0599 / Fax 616-285-3246
e-mail: orders@heritagebooks.org
website: www.heritagebooks.org

ISBN 978-1-60178-140-6

Printed in the United States of America
14 15 16 17 18 19/10 9 8 7 6 5 4 3 2

Journible® Design: Rob Wynalda

Why the 17:18 series?

In Deuteronomy 17, Moses is leaving final instructions concerning the future of Israel. As a prophet of God, Moses foretells of when Israel will place a king over the nation (v. 14). In verses 16 & 17, he lists items that the king could not do as king. In verse 18, he transitions to what he should do as the king.

The king is commanded to not simply acquire a copy of the law (the entire book of Deuteronomy) from the "scroll publishing house," but to hand-write his own copy of the law. The purpose of such a copy written by his own hand was so that:
* he would read it
* he would learn to fear the Lord
* he would obey the commands of God
* his heart would not become proud
* he would not turn to the right or the left from following the law (Prov. 4:27)
* also, his sons would serve in the kingdom after him. (Deut. 17:19,20)

Thirty-four hundred years later, educators are "discovering" that students that physically write out their notes by hand have a much greater retention rate than simply hearing or visually reading the information. Apparently, God knew this to be true of the kings of Israel also.

From such understanding came the conception of this series of books.

Have a great time writing and learning the Word of God,

Rob Wynalda
Romans 1:16

The Purpose of the Journible®

Engagement:

The Journible® is a profoundly simple attempt to aid a person's ability to engage the Word of God by slowing down the process of simply reading the text. The book is organized so that the "scribe" can slowly and thoughtfully engage the text while leaving plenty of room to write comments and questions about the text (Deuteronomy 17:18, Psalms 119, 2 Timothy 3:16,17).

Legacy:

Journibles® provide a legacy to pass on from one generation to the next. The Journible® creates an opportunity for one generation to communicate in writing to the next generation their insights and personal applications of the text (Deuteronomy 6).

How to use this book

This book is organized so that the scribe (you) will hand-write your very own copy of James. You will be writing the text of the Bible only on the right hand page of the book. This should make for easier writing and also allows ample space on the left page of your open text to write your own notes and comments. From time to time a question or word will be lightly printed on the left page; these questions are to aide in further study, but should not interfere with your own notes and comments. This means that you are encouraged to not only write your own "copy" of the Bible, but to also write your own notes concerning the text.

Yes, we are setting aside our mass-produced Gutenberg Bibles and attempting to get back to the simple hand-written copy of the text.

Notes

James

Who is the author and to whom is he writing?

What was the purpose of the letter?

As you "scribe" the book of James, copy verses from the book that you want to remember below.

Notes

(2) Why should trials make you happy?

(5) According to the context of verse 5 what are you asking for wisdom concerning?

1

2

3

4

5

6

7

8

Notes

(14,15) Where does our sin come from?

9

10

11

12

13

14

15

16

Notes

(23,24) What is a person like who does not obey the Word?

17

18

19

20

21

22

23

24

Notes

(26,27) What are the character traits of a truly
religious person?

25

26

27

Notes

(1-7) What is the problem in the church?

1

2

3

4

5

6

7

(8) Look up where the phrase "You shall love your neighbor as yourself" is found in the Bible and explain what it means.

8

9

10

11

12

13

14

15

Notes

(17) How can faith be dead?

16

17

18

19

20

21

22

(23-26) What are the two examples of faith with works and how do they fit in chapter 2?

23

24

25

26

Notes

(2-12) List and explain the metaphors used for the tongue in this section.

1

2

3

4

5

6

7

8

Notes

9

10

11

12

13

14

15

Notes

(16,17) Contrast the by-products of jealousy and wisdom.

16

17

18

Notes

(1) Write out your own answer to the opening question of chapter 4.

1

2

3

4

5

6

7

Notes

(13-15) What is the problem with announcing your future business plans?

8

9

10

11

12

13

14

Notes

(17) What is this verse referring to?

15

16

17

Notes

(1-6) Why should the rich howl?

(7) Therefore — Why should they be patient?

1

2

3

4

5

6

7

Notes

(12) Why is swearing such a problem?

8

9

10

11

12

13

Notes

(17) Look this story up and read it.

14

15

16

17

18

19

20

Notes

Notes

Journibles™ have the look and feel of a classic journal, with a black hard cover, gold foil title, and ribbon bookmark. Just like in this James booklet, right-hand pages feature chapters and verse numbers, which are conveniently spaced according to the length of each verse. Left-hand pages are left blank for your notes and comments on the text. Scattered throughout in light print are questions to guide your thoughts as you study that particular portion of Scripture. As you copy the Scriptures and engage the text in a deeper, more thoughtful way, you will find yourself retaining the truths of God's Word.

Volumes available:
- *Deuteronomy* (352 pages)
- *Proverbs* (224 pages)
- *Psalms 1–72* (336 pages)
- *Psalms 73–150* (368 pages)
- *Luke* (352 pages)
- *John* (256 pages)
- *Acts* (328 pages)
- *Romans* (160 pages)
- *1 & 2 Corinthians* (256 pages)
- *Galatians–2 Thessalonians* (224 pages)
- *1 Timothy–Hebrews* (224 pages)
- *James–Jude* (192 pages)

While Journibles are special tools that will enhance your own personal study of God's Word, here are some other great ways to use them:

- *A lasting legacy for your family*—Include your own special notes about certain passages of Scripture. Your immediate family—and generations to come—will benefit from your insights!

- *Youth ministry*—Use Bible study time to write out Scripture passages, and then discuss them—or assign a passage outside of study time, and discuss it and students' notes when you come together.

- *Small groups*—Leaders assign a passage to write, and then group members come together and discuss their notes.

- *Congregational study*—Pastors challenge church members to write out the text for sermons in advance on right-hand pages and take notes on left-hand pages during the sermon.

- *Discipleship tool*—Spiritually mature believers can use Journibles to shepherd young believers toward spiritual growth.

- *Educational resource*—Good tool for copy work, handwriting practice, reading, and Bible study curriculum.

- *A great gift*—for graduation, birthday, or Christmas. Write your own special note of encouragement inside before you give it away!